Estelle Meaning Star

ESTELLE
MEANING
STAR

Sarah
Rosenthal

chax press
tucson
2024

ISBN 978-1-946104-51-9
Library of Congress Control Number: 2024930092

First Edition 2024

Chax Press
6181 E Fourth St
Tucson AZ 85711
https://chax.org

Chax Press books are supported in part by individual donors
and by sales of books. Please visit *https://chax.org/member-
ship-support/* if you would like to contribute to our mission to
make an impact on the literature and culture of our time.

We thank our current assistants, Erica Cruz and Ben Leitner, for
their work on Chax projects. Our Art Director, Cynthia Miller,
contributes to all books Chax publishes.

Art work on the cover:
Olla Vieja © 2024 Joyce Saler

for stars
and constellations

city and ocean

the women are carrying these

dying dead things

any fear they have

they hide

walking along

pacific rim

I

walking

the rim they

retrieve abandoned animals

wrap arms around

bony torsos

the women tread

slowly   some

carry parasols

shade faces of the dying

dead

walking along

pacific rim

they moan

in lamentation

cradle mangled

animals

4

the women tread the rim

sometimes tear strips

from their dresses

bind around

broken creatures

5

some of them

bend down

gather fistfuls of dirt

rub onto their skin

6

walking the rim

with their bundles of pain

the women gaze down

at stricken eyes

stroke faces

7

the women walk

the women wail

their song of lament

blends with whimpers

of bleeding bodies

slowly they

wend their way

along the narrow path

holding their bleeding

bundles

9

one of our own

signs up for yet

another stint

posting inside papers

about lethargic

TV-watching

10

is a camera

catching me

is crisscross tape

on cement walls

stopping me   are

people hiding

harm in their hands

pools of streetlamp light

snow in the streets

II

pain could thwack me

as I move through

bulging leather wallets

a jittery revolutionary

posting messages

tell them

I've done it

a zillion times I

run at night

straight through the danger

13

messages

must post

about lethargic

watching but danger

strangles sleep

can't keep

up

14

butcher knife

chop myself off

cockeyed with pain

crawl to sit against a far wall

to keep away intruders

stay invisible

people stand before me

hand me a blank card

'have your self give us a call'

cars zooming past

in both directions

15

a folded thing

to her and more

imparts the dictates

of night

executive function

charismatic leader

expected to be feted

'I've been an adventurer

I start every morning

above the sea

tall oak used to be small

knock it cocksure

to table and chairs

a little unstable

muscle discussion'

17

discussion

looking out from balcony

a droplet of wine

in my palm

everyone needs

a new name

because we're all stars

no because we're

another self

positioning

18

position

tell them   say

no I

        I'm an extension

of an official someone

when it's really time for eating

someone will let me

know

19

know how to

squeeze into   language

someone   launches

into confident m—

mistake   stock   still

implies trauma

in light of which

everyone needs

a new name

my   name is Estelle I turn

on my center

speech   freezes

my name is tentatively

she who

21

she who

assume the situation

is playable   try at least

I'm trying

not to I'm trying to   appear

Estelle meaning star

meaning star

trauma table

conversation   all   names are

different versions of the word star

points   and   brilliance

bodies   conferring   against   a

glassy   black

23

night's

middle daughter

disperses

24

bleached hair   animal man   eats in a

dog   way   sunburnt   hands

and   knees   behind a building

on   a little triangular block of open space

this is what someone who's

dead's   doing

someone who's dead's

animal teeth

pink gums above them

not the softness of   hearts

a set of teeth with

nothing to offer

hunched

hunched habits

stalk you

hold your crown like

red-faced animal catchers

dance that high energy dance

dance

learners   appears   there are

two   three but   stare   at

this   number   one

dance hall

gashes along the trapped

people

damage dog

throws itself at door

clatters into room

color running

running girls   found themselves

overlooking the street

party   strode up   inserted

bodies into

conversation   noticed that

pacing animal   it's

incurred a wound

damage dog emitting energy

wounded it

keeps trying to charge the rest of us

over initial shock

girls think it's their job to

inch closer   pick it up

place it under

the table   the dog is

well it's here   they told me

31

while I dream

smell of burnt plastic

from the umbrella

I'd put in the stove

                                    been one
                        oh so
                                sick
to dry
                        cries into claws

was I blind to the dangers

did I feel safe yes perfectly safe

just a casual improvised action

now smoke

32

one hundred fifty broken down

years   broken number now

dead's an improvised happening

won't be needing

legs   elbows   earnest heart

I should feel more left out but I

33

but sweet-faced   hands on my

neck   where's

the first page of my

sheaf I'm

too late for that she responds

suiting herself up

makes a small   cut

incision   squeeze

bitter pellets

from watery pink

tissue

filling many   pages

give things to people

or take things and stuff them in

a crowded well-lit bus

at every stop

moving closer

assignment

walk loud blocks

through crowds

unaware they're words

a phrase or sentence

limps toward me

seems to be my

damage dog

damage dog limps up

wiry with short fur

something stabbed

makes bloodprints

standing on hind legs

places paws   on my shoulders

stare pierces

head presses

against mine whimpering

don't wipe away

this pain

38

this pain

stretches the length of a body

force myself to steady

stay I stay I

stay

torn time

I've thanked

the thin line that showed

skin a world

40

out of eyeshot

no fear but   suicide

the final protest

gleaming tip of another knife

question   invisible

team members

why do you want me to

serve   white   cake

this   sunny morning

please   paper   the   walls

with   notations

carry on a bit in   silence

41

cradling abandoned animals

the women walk

along pacific rim

sometimes they pause

rend shawls   bandage limbs

the women

whisper solace

to the dying dead

proceed

slow stepping

along the rim

43

making their way   to the

far edge   they

carry the   dying   dead

some   crouch

grab   handfuls of   dust

rub   onto   their own

skin

44

making their way

to sea edge

the women

carry the fragile

grieve

45

some adjust

parasols

shade animals

from sunburnt

delirium

in measured

step   they walk

the narrow

ledge   hold

their stricken

charges

drip water

onto parched

tongues

47

they carry mangled

animals to the far

edge   put

the creatures to rest

the women

place the broken

at sea edge

stroke till waves

lap the bones

away

institute a thank you

log a line

didn't exude the proper

excitement as I

ambled to jot down

example

before-the-bell attitude

stank one hundred times

order   stops kids

wandering through hallways

looks deep into

eyes

and they look up what does she want

pants

and skirts

young

and still tied to nature

spiral   root

not sit upright

assignment   settle down

make sure this set

functions   nothing

                     broken or jagged

classroom well outfitted

page well ruled

students   can't see
                        the book
appropriately   from here

face

the teacher

                  dumb

53

dumb

unplanned

out of control

unapproved

work to do

for punishment

mounds of

reading

make sense

make sense

spiral

spring

out of

body of

water

sparkling

breeze

spacious

space

and

54

my   name is Estelle I

turn on my center

I'm   I can't

I'm trying to   rotate

against a glassy black

assume

can be done

        with others

assume discussion

is simple

meaning Estelle

dots the night

and every name

does

does speech   freeze

does mistake imply

trauma   is the situation

playable   how to

          appear

among what's heard

57

does it

I've heard it's

meaning I say   try at least

variations   celestial

bodies constellate

in firmament

confer

try the word star

provisionally she

who all of us

confer in the night

sky Estelle

meaning star

59

say

star

the spark

way   in firmament

points

and brilliance

we visit   style

in three dimensions

layered to prove   effect

trainees enclose

emotion   in waiting

and magic

we keep to our rows

but a child streaks

past architecture

stuffed lamb thrown

onto lawn   lost

sorry touching shoulder

it won't happen again

no discernable sign

all   erupts into chatter

wine pours

lifts a raw canopy

gold lacing through

62

where rooms are also

corridors to pass

structurally impossible setup

when halls are

sunny rooftops

everyone clings to

rectangular restriction

when giveaways

are piled high

hearts help themselves

63

loose confident lines

I'm pouring out some now

one rolls all the way across

sit

here

sit the

previously dreamed version

neighborhood

foldout table

and radical food

mismatched

chairs crowding

against the politicos

tell them

we could hang

a radical panel of

light

the levels are rising

slide toward fantasia

perform this piece

'nevertheless'

'history of anxiety'

'my money'

'mop of tangled glory'

to a still house

67

like in the

dream we have

divining rods

proper and expensive

gathered

at the neck and short sleeves

child where I started

en route to

woman   a destination

jump into the water body

secret moment to wipe

grains from skin

salt I can see

later the late

empties out

tell them

after all these years in the dream

it's a chore

to don clothing

that separated-off feeling

hang gauze over shoulder

come dawn

we'll spin

wild and slow

the dreams   fat silver rings

have decided

for reasons I'm not

privy to to stay   we

dream   jewelry

darker   ray

slides   blind   blythe

hedges a bed   of bushes   through

we're in that   providence   shrubs

garden   public

struck   energy

pitch   forward   perform

darker dream ray   ray

72

tell them   go

pitch your tents

at the edge of

it's late

start

the long trek out

gather here

in the dream

complex and crowding

jammed with

me one after another

amber sun

standard sky

hesitant but I keep pushing for it

twinkling with

Acknowledgements

I am grateful to the editors of the following journals in which
some of these poems have been published: *Word for/Word,
Elderly, Miracle Monacle, Dream Pop,* and *All the Sins.* Thanks to
the Hambidge Center for including the poem beginning "when
rooms are also" in its 2018 *Sign of the Times* exhibit featuring work
by Hambidge Fellows. Gratitude to above/ground press, Dusie
Kollektiv, and Drop Leaf Press, all of which published chapbooks
of selected poems from the manuscript, sometimes in earlier
versions. Thanks to *The Brooklyn Rail* for publishing an interview
about this project with Heidi Van Horn of Drop Leaf Press.

Infinite thanks to all those who loaned me their brilliance along
the way. Jennifer Firestone, Dana Teen Lomax, Denise Newman,
Delia Tramontina, and Erin Wilson gave crucial feedback on the
manuscript-in-progress. Maysie Tift taught me self-hypnosis when
I needed to find my way through a block. Kate Greenstreet,
Joel Gregory, and Jill Magi consulted with me on the logistics of
creating a cut-up book, and Lawrence Arrowsmith and Roberta
Morris contributed invaluable technical skills.

The language in this book is drawn from dream journals written
while undergoing cancer treatment. I am indebted to those who
helped me navigate diagnosis and treatment, including Michael

Alvarado, MD; Jo Chien, MD; Jean Anne Donnell, RN; Emily Flores, NP, MSN; Barbara Fowble, MD; Nima Grissom, MD, FACS; Gretchen Macaire, RD, MA; Martha Sloss, LMFT; Florence Yuen, NP, MSN; and dozens of support staff whose calm, capable presences I leaned on. A heartfelt thank you to family, friends, and colleagues who encircled me with care, and to the utter strangers who treated me so solicitously. These demonstrations of ready compassion taught me so much.

Deep appreciation to Charles Alexander of Chax Press for bringing such remarkable skill and attention to the making of this book, and to Cortney Lamar Charleston, Chris Chen, Carla Harryman, and Camille Roy for their acute and generous readings.

Gratitude to my late mother, Patty Rosenthal, for her fierce encouragement, and to my beloved, Steven Harris, for his tremendous love and support.

About the Author

Sarah Rosenthal is the author of *Estelle Meaning Star* (Chax, 2024), *Lizard* (Chax, 2016), *Manhatten* (Spuyten Duyvil, 2009), and two books in collaboration with Valerie Witte: *One Thing Follows Another: Experiments in Dance, Art, and Life Through the Lens of Simone Forti and Yvonne Rainer* (punctum, 2024) and *The Grass Is Greener When the Sun Is Yellow* (The Operating System, 2019). Her chapbooks include *we could hang a radical panel of light* (Drop Leaf, 2022), *Fire and Flood* (above/ground, 2021), *Estelle Meaning Star* (above/ground, 2014), *disperse* (Dusie, 2014), *The Animal* (in collaboration with artist Amy Fung-yi Lee, Dusie, 2011), *How I Wrote This Story* (Margin to Margin, 2001), *sitings* (a+bend, 2000), and *not-chicago* (Melodeon, 1998). She edited *A Community Writing Itself: Conversations with Vanguard Writers of the Bay Area* (Dalkey Archive, 2010). The film *We Agree on the Sun*, which she made in collaboration with Ayana Yonesaka-Ruiz, Jonah Belsky, and Ames Tierney, was named Best Experimental Short at the Berlin Independent Film Festival. She is the recipient of the Leo Litwak Fiction Award, a Creative Capacity Innovation Grant, a San Francisco Education Fund Grant, and grant-supported writing residencies at This Will Take Time, Hambidge, New York Mills, Vermont Studio Center, Soul Mountain, and Ragdale, as well as a two-year Affiliate Artist term at Headlands Center for the Arts. She is a Life & Professional Coach and a project manager at Collaborative Classroom.

About Chax

Founded in 1984 in Tucson, Arizona, Chax has published more than 240 books in a variety of formats, including hand printed letterpress books and chapbooks, hybrid chapbooks, book arts editions, and trade paperback editions such as the book you are holding. From August 2014 until July 2018 Chax Press resided in the University of Houston-Victoria Downtown Center for the Arts. Chax is a nonprofit 501c3 organization which depends on support from various government & private funders, and, primarily, from individual donors and readers. In July 2018 Chax Press returned to Tucson. In 2021, Chax Press founder and director Charles Alexander was awarded the Lord Nose Award for lifetime achievement in literary publishing. In 2024 Chax established a new studio for its letterpress printing and book arts work.

Our current mailing address is 1517 North Wilmot Road no. 264, Tucson, Arizona 85712-4410. You can email us at *chaxpress@chax.org*

Your support of our projects as a reader, and as a benefactor, is much appreciated.

You may find CHAX at *https://chax.org*

Estelle Meaning Star

has been composed in Gill Sans

with page numbers in Bodoni 72 Oldstyle

Design by Charles Alexander

Image-page design by Sarah Rosenthal

using Cambria as the font for the text in the collages

The cover art work by Joyce Saler was chosen

by Cynthia Miller, Art Director for Chax Press

Printed & Bound by KC Book Manufacturing